Secrets of TikTok Stars

Table of Contents

Collaborate with Other Users
Be Ahead of the Curve
Work Hard
Understand Your Fans

What is TikTok?

TikTok is one of the fastest growing social media platforms on the internet. It boasts 500 million users worldwide, more than Snapchat and Twitter. It's fun to create short videos and share them and to create memes that can go viral. People have used TikTok to create short-form lip-synching videos, #challenges, and sketches.

TikTok is like earlier social media apps like Vine and You Tube, but its 15-second intervals allow users to create funny short videos that are neither as short as those on Vine (6 seconds) or as long as those on You Tube. TikTok users love the authenticity of the platform, on which people can be themselves. They share with their fans things that they would likely only do in the mirror. Most TikTok users are members of Gen Z and are in their teens or early 20s, making the app a showcase for the talents of the younger generation.

The short-form nature of TikTok allows users to be silly and creative and to have some leeway to create their own effects, including sound and filters. Users also like the sense of positive energy the app generates. It's rare for users to provide negative comments.

But beyond having fun and being themselves, people have made serious money on social media platforms, and they have become major influencers who create ads that speak to their audiences. Let's look at some successful TikTokers and see how they created large fan bases. These influencers have shown us that it is possible to gain followers and earn money on social media platforms. Here is a round up of some of their secrets:

Jacob Sartorius

What can you say about this cute megafamous pop star who has risen from Vine and Musical.ly fame to a recording career that has made him millions of dollars?

Jacob, who was adopted and was raised in Virginia, became famous for his lip-synching videos on TikTok, where he has over 21 million followers, before releasing his first single "Sweatshirt."

He made his first Vine about bullying, as he has experienced bullying himself. His intention was not to get likes, he has said, but to create a message about something he cared about. His Vine attracted 15 million followers, as people resonated to his message about kindness.

What we can learn from Jacob is that his message is motivated by what he cares about. He started uploading videos to Vine because he had a message he wanted to share, and he wanted to connect with his audience. People followed him as a result, and they are still following him on his tours.

Baby Ariel

Baby Ariel, a.k.a. Ariel Martin, has gained a huge following on TikTok, with over 29 million followers. She's also gained fans on Instagram, with over 9 million followers, and on You Tube.

Like Jacob Sartorius, Baby Ariel has become a pop sensation, releasing her single "Aww" in 2016 and working on *The Sims 4*. Baby Ariel has devoted herself to anti-bullying, releasing the #ArielMovement, and she is also dedicated to cracking down on online harassment and cyberbullying.

Ariel is dedicated to her fans. She has spoken about feeling close to them and putting out her music in ways that allow fans to react. When she posts her music on social media sites like Instagram and Snapchat, she listens to what her fans have to say about it.

Her advice to budding influencers is to make yourself stand out from the crowd. She advises people to make videos about what interests them-- whether that's sports, or cooking, or something else. She thinks that's the way TikTokers can connect with people who will like their videos.

Baby Ariel also considers herself a kind of cyber big sister. Most of her fans are younger girls, and she is slightly older, allowing her to give them advice and encouragement about growing up and having romantic relationships.

Her secret is also to make a schedule for herself and to post regularly so that she doesn't disappoint her fans.

Jiffpom

This adorable Pomeranian is the most famous pet influencer in the world. After first appearing in a Katy Perry video for "Dark Horse," Jiffpom has gained 30 million followers on different social media platforms. According to the news site Market Watch, this tiny dog makes more money per Instagram post than most humans—he earns about $35 million each time he posts! That's a lot of dog food.

This influencer had his own day in L.A., and Facebook founder Mark Zuckerberg featured Jiffpom at a conference, where the pooch was seated with his own name tag and laptop. He has appeared on TV and in film, and he even won a Guinness World Record for being the fastest dog on front paws. He has a separate record for being the fastest dog on hind legs.

The secret of this pup? He's just so darn cute. It doesn't hurt that he first appeared with Katy Perry in a video that has been seen 2 billion times on YouTube. Jiffpom went where the action was, moving from his home state of Illinois to Los Angeles in 2013. He was willing to give up his front yard in favor of relocating to the city of the stars.

Awez Darbar

Awez is a major influencer who hails from Mumbai, India. He won fame on TikTok and 20 million followers with his funny lip-synching videos, and he also has a large following on Instagram. Awez is a passionate dancer and choreographer who has studied and taught dance. He has even founded his own dance studio.

Awez rocketed to fame through hard work. He has studied dance so that he can improve his moves and choreography, and his hard work has paid off. He is a triple threat, meaning that he is talented in three areas: dancing, choreography, and comedy. His multi-talented nature is what has given him crowned status (on the old TikTok platform).

The Croes Brothers

Gil, short for Gilmer Croes, and his younger brother Jayden hail from the Caribbean island of Aruba. They are one of the top male talents on TikTok. Gil claims over 22 million followers for his funny videos. Jayden, also known as Jay, boasts over 18 million followers.

Gil is an actor and former model, and he has appeared in films. Jay is known for the wave in his hair and for his wigs, hoodies, hats, and other accessories. The brothers clearly like to make people laugh, and their acting talent pays off, as they also have many followers on different social media platforms.

The brothers' secret is that they are good comedians. They know how to make the most of videos by using their expressions and their gestures. They explode on the screen, and it's hard not to laugh alongside them. If you're going to make it on TikTok, it helps to be funny and expressive and to work on your acting skills. Having cool hair doesn't hurt, either.

Jason Coffee and Family

Some influencers on TikTok have transitioned from other social media platforms, such as Jason Coffee and his family. Jason is a former Starbucks barista who made it big on Vine. The father of three children--Peyton, Caleb, and Isaac--he attracts fans with his Christian-inspired family humor. Born in 1980, he is one of the older TikTokers, but he has attracted 2.6 million followers.

His secret: He became famous on Vine after the app was launched in January of 2013 with six-second videos. He then started claiming followers on Musical.ly. His videos, free of vulgarities, feature his family, and many feature family pranks, such as "Kids Dump Eggs Over His Dad's Head Prank." Currently living in Hawaii, he is from Sacramento.

He appeals to families and people who want clean humor. It's possible for people older than Gen Z to be successful on TikTok.

Loren Gray

Loren has over 36 million TikTok fans and 18 million Instagram followers. Her career on Musical.ly launched her into a recording career. Her first single was "My Story," followed by "Kick You Out," in which she sings about the pain of falling in love.

Before launching her music career, she was a vlogger and shared her makeup and beauty tricks with her followers and has been featured in *Seventeen* magazine. Her followers ate up her beauty tips, including how to create her super-long eyelashes, and she shared crush advice in a video with HRVY.

What's her secret? It doesn't hurt that she served up major beauty tricks, and she lets her followers in on them. Her followers got to know her before she turned to her music career.

Tips for TikTokers

Here are some tips for getting the best shots and material uploaded on TikTok and getting people to follow you.

Camera Work

Many TikTokers are tempted to film using hand-held phones, but this won't always allow the best shots. Instead, use a tripod to make sure you have smooth camera work that's not jumpy. Consider the best angles for your shots, and don't forget about lighting.

You can shoot your videos in your bedroom if you think that's the right place, but consider whether another location might be better. For example, some people have filmed to good effect in malls or outdoors.

Experiment with speeds, like slo-mo. The slo-mo hair flip is a cool trick, but if you don't feel comfortable with effects, start with the regular speed first before you move into special effects.

Creating Transitions

Holly H has some really helpful videos on YouTube that explain how she creates transitions in her videos. For one type of transition, she swings her arm around to the back of her head. In another, she films in fast mode and then slows down and moves her phone to the center of the frame.

It takes some practice to master these moves, and she shows you how to do them while holding your phone. She also shows you the effect of these transitions.

The Look of Your Work

Your videos should look good. You should also look good in your videos. Do you notice how a lot of influencers have good hair and clothes? If you're going for comedy, you can still style yourself before appearing before the camera. Try to cultivate a signature look so that your fans know you and know what to expect from you (this doesn't mean you can change it up sometimes, though).

Use Hashtags

Make sure you are current with the top hashtags on TikTok. Check out what is trending on the app, and use those hashtags. A good one is always #tik-tok or #love. People post the top hashtags, so you can stay current and attract more fans.

Try to use more than one hashtag so that you are more likely to attract attention from people looking for a certain hashtag that is trending on the front page.

Don't Shy Away from Challenges

The challenges on TikTok can also help you attract fans. People look for different responses to the challenges. Try to create unique, different content for the challenges, and your videos will be more visible.

Look Good

People who attract a lot of fans tend to look good. They groom themselves before appearing on camera, and they practice facial expressions and acting techniques. Before recording your video, make sure you apply makeup and brush your hair. Videos with more attractive people tend to get more views. Don't worry if you're not ready for the cover of a magazine. Just look neat and clean.

The short form of TikTok videos rewards people who can show expressive gestures to the camera. Work on your acting and facial expressions so that you can convey a lot of emotion to the camera.

Be Consistent

Don't just post one video and expect to be famous. Instead, keep posting on a regular basis and build your fans slowly over time. Before you start, you may want to make about 10 videos and keep posting them to the app so that you can continue to attract fans. If people like your videos, they will continue to want more, so be sure to keep up your work and let your fans know that you are there for them.

Use Social Media Platforms

Connect with your fans on more than one platform. Post your videos to YouTube and Instagram to draw people to your TikTok videos. Connect with other people by liking their work and following them, and this will encourage them to follow your work too. Remember that TikTok is about positive energy and sharing the love, not abusing others. It's the most positive social media site out there right now, so keep it loving and real.

Collaborate with Other Users

If you can team up with someone who has a similar number of fans, you can create a duet with them. That way, you can get some of their fans to follow your videos as well. This can be a way for you to share fans with the other person and to generate more fans for yourself as well.

Be Ahead of the Curve

Try to jump on sounds when they are beginning to trend. Find a sound that is beginning to be popular and use it in your videos. Try not to wait until the sound is too popular, or there will be too many videos with that sound. The idea is to be ahead of the curve a bit, so you can catch the wave and ride it towards popularity--and more fans.

Post at the Right Time

The best time to post is during the day, not at night. That's because there are more people on the app during the day, so if you post during those hours, you will get more likes from fellow Tik-Tokers. Try to time your videos so that you're uploading them during the day time.

Work Hard

The famous TikTokers didn't reach stardom overnight. They worked hard on the look of their videos, on their dancing and choreography, and their results did not come overnight. To improve your videos, look into what the stars are doing right.

One element that successful videos have in common is that the creators know their audiences well. They have found a niche, or a style or subject that helps them connect with their fans. For example, if you are a comedian, work hard on improving your comedic skills and understanding what your audience likes. Study other videos that are funny and discover what they have that you don't. Work on your acting skills and look into acquiring props that set you apart from others.

Understand Your Fans

This is perhaps the most important step you can take. Pay attention to your fans' feedback--what they like and what they don't. For example, Jason Coffee has successfully used clean comedy to appeal to fans of family humor. He understands who his audience is. Baby Ariel knows that her fans are mostly tween and teen girls who look up to her as an older sister figure, and they trust her advice. Loren Gray began to appeal to her fans first by giving them advice about makeup and beauty.

Your fans need to feel that they can count on you and that you will upload videos regularly and consistently. They also need to feel that you know their tastes and what they like or find funny. That doesn't mean that you can't occasionally try something new and see how it works with your fan base, but try to keep your fans interested and related to you by giving them what they like on a regular basis.

What's the ideal number of videos you should post? Posting once per week is definitely not enough if you are trying to get fans. Probably posting once per day is about right. If possible, you can try to post different types of videos twice a day. That way, you can create a more interesting mix.

Good luck and have fun!

www.ingramcontent.com/pod-product-compliance
Lightning Source LLC
Chambersburg PA
CBHW031249050326
40690CB00007B/1028